EARTH MAN!
Day 6

PAPA & MAMA GOOSE

EARTH MAN! – DAY 6

Papa & Mama Goose

Copyright © 2020
Enchanted Rose Publishing
P.O. Box 991
Hempstead, TX 77445

Published by Enchanted Rose Publishing
Layout by Cynthia D. Johnson @
www.diverseskillscenter.com

Written by Papa & Mama Goose

Printed in the United States of America
ISBN-13: 978-1-947799-66-0

It was a day like no other...Day 6 of The Creation.

The sun had finally made its way to shine its glory upon Earth's face as she slept through the night.

The moon and stars packed their bags and headed-off to the next planet.

The plants basked in the brilliance of the sunlight as it provided the plant life daily nourishment.

The first portion of the day would begin with GOD creating living creatures after their species.

There were cattle, creeping things, and beasts of the earth.

Can you picture in your mind's eye, sheep, zebras, and bears living in harmony with one another?

Because there was no sin on the earth, the animals did not harm or eat each other.

If I could go back into time, I can almost see the animals getting the memo that GOD would be creating His biggest miracle EVER today.

All the animals would be about their day, business as usual, longing to be the first to see what would come after their own incredible existence.

I can imagine that GOD the Father, GOD the SON, and GOD the HOLY SPIRIT discussing how they would create man.

They took the dust of the earth, shaped it, and created the inner and outer man.

After the man was made, he laid there.

As if he was in a deep sleep, the man was lifeless and unresponsive.

By this time, the grapevine had begun.

I can envision one animal telling another, and so on, and so forth.

I think you get the picture.

Perhaps the animals were excited and anticipating what GOD would do with the man lying on the ground.

In my mind's eye, I can see the animals watching intently...wondering what GOD was going to do next.

According to the Bible, GOD said, "Let us make man in our image and after our likeness. And let them have dominion over the fish of the sea, fowl of the air, and over the cattle, and over all the earth, and over every creeping thing that creepeth upon the earth."

GOD breathed His breath into the man's nostrils.

Suddenly, the man's heart began to beat.

His eyes were opened.

The man became a living soul...he was alive!!!

I'm sure if the animals were actually watching GOD create Adam, they could hardly contain themselves.

They must have known that GOD had given them their leader and king.

GOD called the man he made Adam.

While living in the Garden of Eden, Adam was given the responsibility of caring for the garden.

Adam was brilliant and equipped with a photogenic memory.

Did you know that GOD brought all the animals to Adam to be given a name?

Imagine what we could do for GOD when we utilize all the gifts and talents He has given us!

Day in and day out, Adam began noticing something.

He noticed that all the animals had mates, except him.

GOD wanted Adam to know that he too would need a companion to help him in the world in which he lived.

So, GOD created a woman from Adams's rib and brought the woman to the man.

GOD commanded Adam and Eve to be fruitful and multiply.

They were commanded to subdue the earth and everything in it.

Finally, GOD instructed man and every creature to eat herbs for their meat.

No animal had to worry about being on fast food menu during the time of Adam.

GOD looked on all

He had made and

called it good.

Genesis 1: 24-31;

Genesis 2:20-25

Follow Me On...

 **Facebook**

www.facebook.com/goma
magoose

 **Twitter**

@GoMamaGoose

 **Instagram**

MamaGoose Paris
gomamagoose@gmail.com

Papa & Mama Goose Media

Through the power of their faith and instructions from GOD's HOLY SPIRIT, these humble servants of CHRIST take us back to our beginning...The Bible. Although Papa and Mama Goose have written a plethora of books, none can hold a candle to how the WORD of GOD has guided their lives. Realizing that life on Earth is temporal, Papa and Mama Goose wanted to write Books about the Bible that would provide a Biblical Foundation for young children. The goal of the books is to teach youngsters to know and fall deeply in Love with GOD.

It was during their years in college that Papa and Mama Goose found CHRIST. They were taught the Gospel and baptized into the Prairie View CHURCH of CHRIST at Prairie View A & M University in Prairie View, Texas. Papa and Mama Goose enjoy sharing the same spiritual birthday. Currently, the dynamic duo are faithful members of the Fifth Ward CHURCH of CHRIST in Houston, Texas.

www.ingramcontent.com/pod-product-compliance
Lightning Source LLC
Chambersburg PA
CBHW041238040426
42445CB00004B/69